LOST

When the Dream turns to a Nightmare

Jonty Allcock

Lost: When the Dream Turns to a Nightmare

The Good Book Company
Tel: 0333-123-0880; International: +44 (0) 208 942 0880
Email: admin@thegoodbook.co.uk

Websites:
UK: www.thegoodbook.co.uk
N America: www.thegoodbook.com
Australia: www.thegoodbook.com.au
New Zealand: www.thegoodbook.co.nz

This book is based on a series of talks given at *Sorted* 2009, organised by Capital Youthworks. www.capitalyouthworks.com

ISBN: 9781907377228

Design and illustration: André Parker
Printed in the UK

Contents

Introduction

Now the tax collectors and "sinners" were all gathering around to hear him [Jesus]. But the Pharisees and the teachers of the law muttered, "This man welcomes sinners and eats with them."

Luke 15 v 1-2

I am thirty three years old. I would like to be able to say that in those thirty three years I have made a remarkable impact on human history. But I haven't. According to Facebook I have managed to pick up some friends along the way. I have passed some exams (and failed some too). I can juggle. I have a badge that says I can swim five metres with water wings. Remarkable? Not exactly.

You will be glad to know this book is not about me. This book is all about. ***Jesus***.

He lived on this earth for about thirty three years. In those thirty three years he turned the world upside down. His short life is the centre point of human history. By any standard he lived a remarkable life. Millions of people around the world follow him and call him King. In this book I want us to work out what all the fuss is about.

We're going to look at one of the stories Jesus told. It's a story that will bring us face to face with the real Jesus. Are you ready to meet him?

The story is very simple. One dad; two sons; living on a farm. But don't be fooled into thinking it is a nice little fairytale. It is explosive. Some people who heard it the day that Jesus first told it became very angry. They were left muttering and grumbling. They found this story deeply offensive. They hated Jesus for it. Hated him so much that they wanted to kill him.

But other people listening in the crowd were blown away by this simple story. It was the most breathtaking thing they had ever heard.

So before we get started, let me give you a warning. This story might make you very angry. Or it might make your heart burn with joy. It is powerful stuff. Are you sure you are ready?

What Jesus is telling us in this story can be summed up in four words:

This man welcomes sinners.

That is the accusation that is chucked at Jesus by the religious leaders of the day. They are not happy. Huge numbers of people are travelling miles to come and listen to what Jesus has to say about God. By itself that would make the religious leaders jealous. But these aren't the good guys who are turning up. Jesus is surrounded by a seriously dodgy crowd of people. They are the sinners, the tax collectors—basically another name for thieves in those days—the bad boys. And Jesus doesn't seem to be bothered. In fact, he seems pleased to see them. There is no getting away from it. Jesus is making friends with them. He is welcoming sinners.

But Jesus hears this muttering at the back of the crowd and tells this story to answer them.

In a very powerful way Jesus says to them: "Yes, you are right, I do welcome sinners".

This is what Jesus is all about. This is the reason he came.

In a world where acceptance so often depends on how pretty you are, how slim you are, how good you are, how well you keep the rules, how rich you are, how brainy you are, how… whatever you are, here is some good news:

This man welcomes sinners.

In a world where many people feel guilty and worthless and unlovable, here is some good news:

This man welcomes sinners.

Come with me and experience the power and emotion of this surprising story for yourself. Come and meet the man who welcomes sinners.

Chapter One:
Pursue the dream!

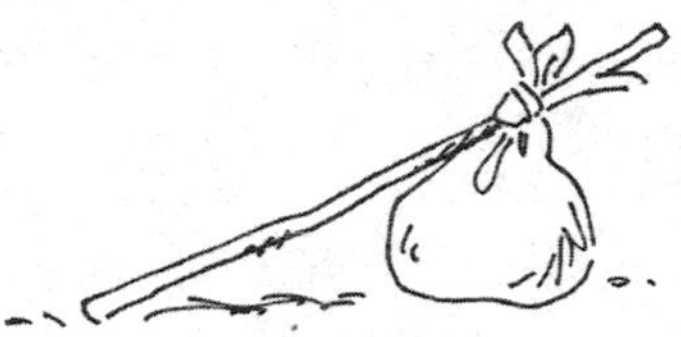

Jesus continued: "There was a man who had two sons. The younger one said to his father, 'Father, give me my share of the estate.' So he divided his property between them. Not long after that, the younger son got together all he had, set off for a distant country and there squandered [wasted] his wealth in wild living."

Luke 15 v 11-13

I used to hate Friday afternoons. One hundred minutes of maths stretched out ahead of me. It was a terrible way to end each week. As the minutes ticked s-l-o-w-l-y by I knew I was in a struggle for survival. I tried doodling little pictures all over my maths folder (vaguely satisfying—for the first three minutes). I tried sleeping with my eyes open (not very easy, try it sometime). I tried listening to what the teacher was saying (radical, I know, but things were desperate). It was no good. There was nowhere to hide. It was official; my life was utterly boring.

So I allowed my mind to drift away and I began to dream. I dreamed about what my life could be. I dreamed about releasing my first single. I dreamed about presenting children's TV (don't tell anyone that). I dreamed about a masked gunman bursting into the classroom and how I would risk my life to save my friends (does that make me strange?) and… then the bell rang.

It isn't hard to see why we spend so much time daydreaming. It feels like there must be more to life than our boring little existence. We watch the latest Hollywood film and we can't help but feel we're missing out. We watch TV talent shows and see another person's dream come true and it is so annoying. Everyone else in the world seems to be having so much fun, but we feel trapped in our dull little world.

"What if?… I wonder… If only…" we say to ourselves.

Some of us dream huge dreams. Things like winning the lottery, playing in the World Cup, or getting a record deal. Some of us are slightly less ambitious. We dream of passing exams, or getting a girlfriend, or learning to drive.

Whatever it might be, we all dream of a better life with more excitement or money or happiness.

And those dreams can be extremely powerful. They promise to satisfy us and make us happy. They promise to put an end to the boredom. They promise us life as it is meant to be lived. They promise to quench our thirst and give us meaning.

So what's your daydream?

A boy with a dream

In Luke 15 Jesus tells a brilliant story. It starts with a young man. A young man with a dream.

He lives on a farm with his dad and older brother. One big happy family. It all looks so perfect.

Or perhaps not. The younger son is fed up of life on Old MacDonald's farm and is dreaming of bigger and better things. He has ambition; he doesn't want to spend the rest of life cleaning up after cows.

You can imagine how the thought first began to grow in his head. Everyday he gets up and goes out to work. He has to do whatever his dad says. He has to work hard. He feels like a slave. It is official. His life is boring. And so, as he digs the land, his mind drifts away. The dream begins to take hold.

He dreams of the day he can pack his bags and head to the city. He dreams of the fun he will have. He dreams of the women, the parties, the laughter. He dreams of freedom.

But, there is one slight problem. There is an obstacle standing in the way of his dream. His dad. While his dad is alive, he cannot leave. While his dad is alive, the younger son has no money of his own. But once the old man dies, then he will be rich. So all he has to do is wait. And wait. He is waiting for his dad to die.

You can almost imagine the disappointment on his face each day as he comes down to breakfast and finds his father has made it through another night. "Still alive then, dad?"

This boy has no love for his father; that much is very clear. All that matters to him is his powerful dream. As the days drag on, the house becomes more like a prison. How long will he have to live this boring life? How long before he can get away? He feels trapped. Until one day he snaps; he cannot take it any more. He makes his choice.

He dumps his dad and pursues his dream.

Dumped

Being dumped is a terrible feeling. And, when you think about it, saying "You've been dumped" is a pretty harsh way to split up with a girlfriend or boyfriend. I remember once finding one of my friends crying his eyes out behind the bike racks because he had just been dumped. You feel like a bit of worthless rubbish being chucked away.

That's what the son does to his dad. He dumps him. He treats him like a bit of old junk; then he simply walks away. He is free at last. He has dumped his dad. Now he can pursue the dream.

This is shocking stuff. He has done a terrible thing. Take a closer look at how the son treats his dad. Three words sum it up: grabbing, leaving, wasting.

Grabbing

He grabs. He comes to his dad with an outrageous request. "Father, give me my share of the estate." Not a word of thanks; not a hint of respect. Just a grubby little hand outstretched to grab what he can.

He's acting like a typical three-year-old. Toddlers have a very simple method of getting what they want. They just grab it. We've all seen it happen. They see someone else with a toy that looks like fun. They want it. They toddle over, take hold, snatch it, then they run away with the loot. Fast. The helpless victim is left crying. It is not pretty. No parent says: "How cute, he just snatched that toy." In fact it is downright ugly.

The younger son in our story is using the classic three-year-old strategy. He knows what he wants and he's going to get it. He toddles over and grabs it. It is not pretty. It is very obvious that he doesn't love his father. In fact, he would prefer it if his dad was dead.

Leaving

His next move is to run away. He puts as much distance as he can between himself and his father. He walks away from the house, he walks away from his boring life, he walks away from his dad.

As the boy walks off into the distance, he has his head held high. This is his moment. This is his destiny.

You could sum him up in the words of a Burger King advert:

> ***"You have the right to have what you want, exactly when you want it. Because on the menu of life, you are "today's special". And tomorrow's. And the day after that. And... Well, you get the drift. Yes, that's right. We may be the king, but you, my friend, are the mighty ruler."***

Our boy is feeling the freedom. He has got exactly what he wants. He is the mighty ruler.

But in the father's heart there is a deep pain. He has been dumped. The son doesn't even say goodbye.

Wasting

The run-away son arrives in the city. We're told that he wastes the wealth in wild living. He wastes it all. He has no limits; he can do exactly what he wants. We aren't told exactly what he gets up to but he is living the dream. At last he has broken free from the shackles of home. He doesn't have to get up and go to work. He doesn't have to do what his dad says. He's free. With every coin he spends, he's showing his absolute rejection of his dad: the money his dad had worked hard to save; the money his dad has lovingly stored up to provide for his family. Our boy couldn't care less about that. He just keeps spending and spending and spending till it's all gone.

Are you shocked by what this son does? You should be. He's done a terrible thing.

But hold on a second. Don't miss the point of all this. Jesus wants us to see that we've all treated God in exactly the same way. Shocking? It should be.

We all have a dream

The story of the human race is one of dumping God in order to pursue our own dreams. Right back at the start of the Bible we find the first man and woman doing exactly that. They were lovingly created by God. They were given a beautiful world to enjoy. They were designed to live under God's loving rule.

But they had their own dreams. In Genesis 3 we read about how they began to daydream. They wanted to be like God. They were dreaming of wisdom, they were dreaming of freedom. Being under God's rule began to seem a bit restricting. How much better it would be if they could rule themselves. Then they could live their own way rather than God's. It was a powerful dream.

But there was one slight problem. There was an obstacle standing in the way of their dream.

God.

They faced a choice. Which way would they go?

They dumped God and pursued their own dream.
The Bible says they took what they had been told they could not have. They grabbed. They snatched. They toddled over, took hold of it and pulled.

That's been the story of the human race ever since. Ever since the first man and woman dumped God, we have all followed along.

There is another part of the Bible that puts it like this.

> ***No one is right with God, no one at all. No one understands. No one trusts in God. All of them have turned away...***
> ***Romans 3 v 10-12 (NIRV Bible translation)***

These are shocking words. All human beings have dumped God in order to pursue our own dreams. This is what the Bible calls sin. It is an ugly and terrible thing. Grabbing what we can from God. Leaving him far behind and wasting the things he gives us on ourselves.

We often try and pretend sin is no big deal. I am just having fun. I'm not harming anyone. Chill out, stop worrying about God and enjoy yourself.

This story helps us face up to the truth about sin. Every time I sin, I am dumping God to pursue my dream. It is that serious.

Every day I face the choice—will I follow what God says or what I want (my "dreams")?

Perhaps you sometimes feel like this...

> ***You have the most unreasonable parents in the whole world. You are convinced that their sole aim in life is to spoil yours. You want to let fly and tell them what you really think of them. You're sure it would make you feel better. But God says that we should honour our parents. You face the choice. If you're going to follow your dream, you have to dump God first.***

"I'm 52-honest!"

> ***You're under age and you want to go clubbing with your mates. Surely it is no big deal to lie about your age to the doorman. Everyone does it. But God loves truth and he wants us***

to love truth too. You face the choice. If you are going to follow your dream, you have to dump God first.

God says that sex is a brilliant gift to be enjoyed within marriage. But you're in love and your boyfriend has asked you to sleep with him. You're sure it will make you happy. You face the choice. If you are going to follow your dream, you have to dump God first.

You're football crazy. It's all you talk about, think about, dream about. In fact football is taking over everything. If you worked hard, you might even get to play in the World Cup. But God says that we should love him more than anything else in the world. You face the choice...

Wait. Hold on. Stop. Stop. Stop.

God is sounding like a real old spoil-sport; like a cosmic policeman in the sky ready to hand out a fine to anyone who smiles.

No way!

God loves you. He designed you. He made you. He gave you life. He wants you to be happy. Really happy. We can only see our dreams. But he can see where our dreams are really leading us to.

More than that, he is also the God who created the whole universe. The Rightful King. The All-Powerful Ruler. And every day we dump him for our own little desires.

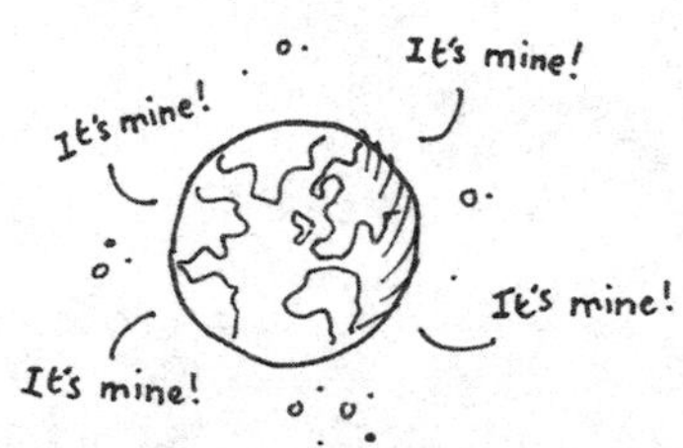

We need to stop pretending that these things don't matter. They really do.

More to life than dreams?

The problem is not that our daydreams are too big. Actually, it's that they are too small!

You were not made to pursue your own dreams. You were made for something far bigger, far more exciting and far more important.

You were made to pursue God.

Here are some words from the Bible in Psalm 63. Look at what this guy says he is living for:

> ***God, you are my God.***
> ***I greatly long for you.***
> ***With all my heart I thirst for you***
> ***in this dry desert***
> ***where there isn't any water.***
>
> ***Psalm 63 v 1 (NIRV translation)***

He can see that the world is dry and weary. It's like a desert that will only leave us thirsty. It will never satisfy our thirst for the important things in life.

So instead he is longing for God. What is the result? He tells us a few sentences later.

> ***I will be as satisfied as if I had eaten the best food there is.***

The satisfaction you are longing for is not to be found in your daydreams of money, fame or success. You are designed to find your satisfaction in God. He is the One we are supposed to be seeking. He is the One we should desire. He is the One we are to long for. Anything less than that and we are missing out. More on this in chapter two…

Take a moment to think about your own dreams. What are they? Can you write them down?

In what ways have you dumped God in the past week in order to run after what you think will make you happy?

Perhaps you could talk to God about it now…

Chapter Two:

Crash landing!

He spent everything he had. Then the whole country ran low on food. So the son didn't have what he needed. He went to work for someone who lived in that country, who sent him to the fields to feed the pigs. The son wanted to fill his stomach with the food the pigs were eating. But no one gave him anything.

Then he began to think clearly again. He said, "How many of my father's hired workers have more than enough food! But here I am dying from hunger! I will get up and go back to my father." *Luke 15 v 14-20 (NIRV translation)*

No one likes being lied to. When I was fourteen I bought a portable TV from a bloke in the market. "Give me five for it," he said. "It's my last one, and I want to go home." What a bargain! The man promised me it was top quality. It was unbelievably cheap. I was so excited. But when I got it home, the box was empty. I'd been conned. I paid good money for a cardboard box full of… more cardboard. I was so disappointed, and I felt like a complete muppet for being taken in.

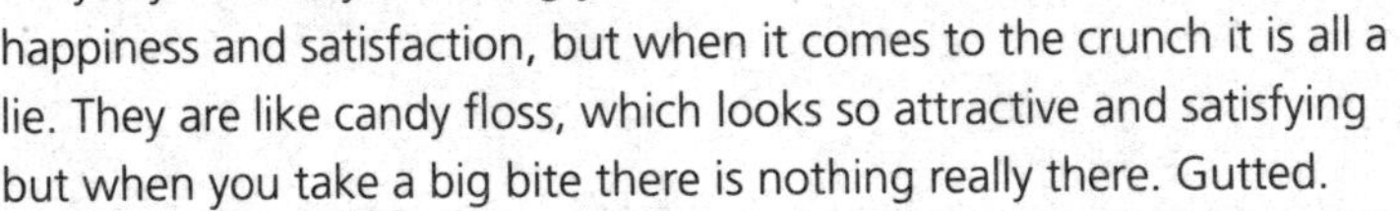

We are in danger of being conned by our daydreams. Do you realise that your daydreams are lying to you? They make big promises, and great claims. They say that they can bring you happiness and satisfaction, but when it comes to the crunch it is all a lie. They are like candy floss, which looks so attractive and satisfying but when you take a big bite there is nothing really there. Gutted.

Your daydreams are lying.

That is what our boy in the story is about to find out. We left him living the dream: wild parties, everything you could ever hope for. But suddenly the bubble bursts, the party is over and the dream becomes a nightmare. His life starts to nose dive out of control; you can feel the desperation as the whole dream falls apart before his eyes. Let's zoom in for a closer look at the way it all comes crashing down.

Gurgle, gurgle

We are told that the boy spent everything he had. In other words the money has run out. Like your bath water disappearing down the drain, his last few coins have gurgled away and his wallet is empty. You can see the problem: as his money disappears into the plumbing, so does his dream. It was his dad's money that fuelled his party lifestyle. As soon as the money is gone, the dream goes with it.

Think about that for a moment. Jesus is giving us a wake-up call in our money-crazy culture. We're obsessed with money. We work hard so we can get a good job. We want a good job so we can get plenty of money. And we want plenty of money because…?

It's simple. It's because money is the key that unlocks the door to our daydreams. Money is the genie that makes wishes come true. That's why money is so powerful. We worship money because we worship anything that offers us happiness.

But this boy learned the tough way that money doesn't deliver. Don't get me wrong; money can make you happy. It can get you a nice house and car. It can deliver you a party lifestyle. It can make you very happy—for a while. It may give you some of the things you want. But it will never deliver what we really need deep down—the things that will give us deep joy and satisfaction.

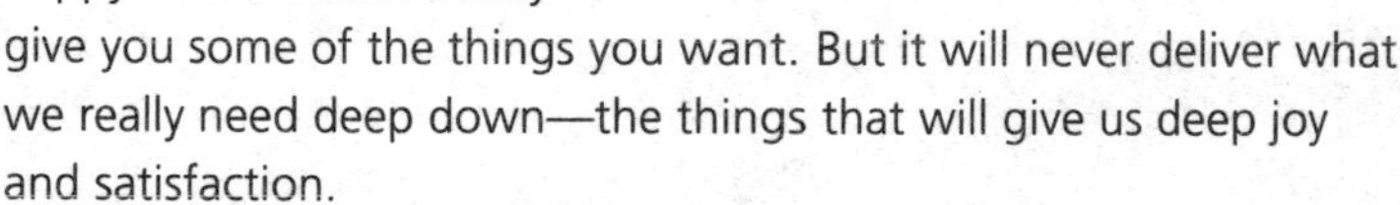

And at some point, money will let you down. You'll find that you don't have enough. You'll find that you are trapped by a continual need for more and more. You'll find your life dominated and controlled. And at the end of it all money will fail you. In the face of death, its power will run out. It's promises will come crashing down. You will leave it all behind. Don't fall for the lie. Don't be conned.

The money runs out, but the worst is yet to come…

Rumble, rumble

A famine hits the country. Now our boy is in big trouble. He left home so full of self-belief and pride. But how things have changed. For the first time in his life he is in need. He was used to having plenty of food and a warm bed at home. He'd lived it rich when he had his pockets full of his dad's money. But not anymore. The sound of laughter has been replaced by the sound of a rumbling stomach.

No longer is his head full of grand ideas and crazy dreams – all he cares about is where his next mouthful is going to come from. Life has become a matter of survival. He's been completely humbled.

What is it they say? Pride comes before a fall?

Incredibly he still has further to fall...

Crash!

He needs money and he needs it fast. If he could find a job, he could begin to turn his life around. So he goes to work for a local farmer—it's the job he knows how to do. But do you see how crazy this is? He left the warmth, comfort and family of his dad's farm because he had convinced himself it was "slavery" and he was dreaming of freedom. But he ends up a as... a real slave... on a farm.

It keeps getting worse. He is sent to a field to feed pigs. No choice. No arguments. No option. He has to get on with it.

This is a spectacular crash landing. It doesn't get any lower than this. Jews and pigs just did not hang out together. To be in contact with a pig made you ceremonially unclean (that means filthy in God's eyes). Being unclean meant you were unfit for God and unfit for His people. So there he is. With the pigs. Filthy. Hopeless. Despairing.

He's hungry. And no one gives him anything. He is so desperate he is even jealous of the pigs. It is so depressing. A bunch of smelly pigs are doing better in life than he is.

He's chased after happiness but only run into misery. The pleasure he wanted has ended up in emptiness. He's far from home. He's far from God. He's lost.

Before we feel sorry for him, just remember why he's actually in with the pigs. He had a great home, plenty of food, a loving father; and he dumped it all to pursue his dream. This is the life he chose. A life without dad. A life of "freedom". But his daydreams were lying to him. They could never deliver on what they promised.

Don't be conned

This is a serious warning about the dangers of chasing your dreams. It may feel right. It may seem wise. It may be great fun. But it's always heading for a crash landing. At the end of the day your dreams cannot deliver on what they promise. They will lead you to slavery. You will be lost.

You were not made to pursue your own dreams. You were made to pursue God. You are designed to desire him; you are wired to worship him; that is the highest purpose in your life. Life does not get any better than that. Anything less will always leave us feeling empty. When we dump God to pursue our dream, we are simply left hungry and alone, with filthy pigs for company.

This desperate desire to pursue our dreams is ruining millions of people across our world. And Jesus is brutally honest with us. We need to WAKE UP and smell the pig filth. Life is not all about me. It is not all about my dreams. It is not all about what I want. There is something so much bigger.

God will not allow proud human beings to go on dumping him and pursuing the dream. He will bring them crashing down. Another part of the Bible written by a man called James says: "God opposes the proud".

You can see it all through the Bible. Again and again. Visit the Tower of Babel in Genesis 11. Go and look at what happened when human beings dumped God to pursue the dream of building a massive building to make a name for themselves. He came down to stop them.

Go to the Hanging Gardens of Babylon in Daniel 4. Go and look at what happened to proud King Nebuchadnezzar as he looked at the mighty city he had built. God humbled him and sent him away to eat grass with the cows.

Go and visit the palace in Jerusalem in Acts 12. Look at what happened to proud King Herod, who was sitting on his throne acting as though he was God. He became food for the worms.

It is always the same. Dumping God and chasing our dreams always ends up in a crash landing.

A glimmer of hope

Our boy is in a mess. His dream is in tatters, but then he makes his first wise move of the story. He doesn't settle for the pig food. Instead he starts to use his brain. Jesus says that the boy began to think clearly again. At last he is starting to *think*. He stops pretending and starts to face reality.

He begins to think again about his father. He begins to think about his home. He remembers where he belongs. He starts to feel homesick. He had to fall a long way to get to this point. But now he is ready to go back.

You may have hit rock bottom. You might feel hopeless. It might seem that your life is too messed up ever to be put straight. If that's you, then start to think. Think about where your dreams have got you. Face up to the reality. No excuses. No self pity, just an honest look at life. Then, keep thinking. It is so important that you don't settle for a shattered dream. You were created for so much more. Don't give up. Don't despair.

Keep thinking—now think about God.

Think about the God who created you and loves you. Think about the empty daydreams you've been pursuing. Think about how stupid it is to have dumped the only person who truly knows what's best for you. Think about...

Are you ready to return to God? It's simple to do. You just talk to him. From wherever you are. Admit what you have done. Say sorry.

In the next chapter, we'll find out what happens when we do.

You may be reading this and life is good. Pursuing your dreams seems to be going great. If that's you, then start to think about how fragile your life really is. Start to think—about God. You don't have to wait to hit rock bottom before you return to God.

Take some time to honestly examine your dreams now. Can you write down what they are promising you? Can they really deliver what they are promising?

Ask God to help you not to be conned by the daydreams, but to see things clearly.

Why not talk to God about it now…?

Chapter Three: Welcome home

When he came to his senses, he said, 'How many of my father's hired men have food to spare, and here I am starving to death! I will set out and go back to my father and say to him: Father, I have sinned against heaven and against you. I am no longer worthy to be called your son; make me like one of your hired men.' So he got up and went to his father.

But while he was still a long way off, his father saw him and was filled with compassion for him; he ran to his son, threw his arms around him and kissed him.

The son said to him, 'Father, I have sinned against heaven and against you. I am no longer worthy to be called your son.'

But the father said to his servants, 'Quick! Bring the best robe and put it on him. Put a ring on his finger and sandals on his feet. Bring the fattened calf and kill it. Let's have a feast and celebrate. For this son of mine was dead and is alive again; he was lost and is found.' So they began to celebrate.

Luke 15 v 17-24

What happens next in the story might just blow your mind. It is stunning and breathtaking and awe inspiring and extraordinary and stupendous and jaw dropping and heart thumping and…

That is no exaggeration. It really is that good.

Don't read this chapter if you are feeling sleepy. Save it for when you are awake. Please don't rush this. Take time to allow the emotion of the story to sink in. This is a story about Jesus and about you. Don't miss that.

Why not talk to God before you start? Ask him to show you who Jesus really is and what he is like. He's the man who welcomes sinners.

Here we go.

The boy is on his way home. He is not feeling good about himself. The last time he saw his dad was to grab his money and leave. He shudders now as he remembers how harsh his words were to his dad. He can still see the pain in his father's eyes. Now he is on his way home.

What will happen when he knocks on the door? He deserves nothing. In fact, he deserves to be seriously punished.

There is just one small hope. Maybe, just maybe, his father will allow him to work as a slave. He could earn some money, begin to pay back his father.

He knows he is not worthy to ever be called "son" again, but perhaps his dad will show him mercy and give him work. Anything would be better than the emptiness and hunger of the pig sty. He has his speech worked out: "Father, I have sinned against heaven and against you. I am no longer worthy to be called your son; make me like one of your hired men."

He isn't coming with excuses or demands, just a faint hope that his father will show him some kindness.

He knows the chances are slim; it's a long shot. But he has nowhere else to turn. If his dad turns him away, he will almost certainly starve.

He makes his way home. Imagine him turning the final corner, catching sight of the house in the distance. Imagine his heart beating, his mouth going dry. What sort of a welcome is waiting for him?

Nothing could have prepared him for what was about to happen.

A mind-blowing welcome

Back in the house is an old man. The father who had been dumped. A man whose eyes have wept many tears and whose heart has experienced much pain. A man whose eyes even now are sweeping the horizon for a glimpse of his boy.

Then, suddenly he sees something; there's a man walking towards the house. Is it him? It can't be, can it? He looks too thin and dirty. But wait. Yes it is him. It's his boy; his precious son; he's coming home!

Jesus says that the sight of his lost son in the distance causes something to happen inside the father. He is filled with compassion. His heart explodes with love for the lonely figure trudging wearily down the road towards him.

And we mustn't miss the shock of this. It is an extraordinary reaction in the heart of the father. After all he has been through.

He doesn't know why the boy is returning. For all he knows he might be coming back for more money. We might at least expect the father to wait and make sure the boy is really sorry. To make him suffer a bit. But there is none of that in the father.

Without a moment's hesitation he is off. He hitches up his robe and legs it towards the boy. He doesn't wait to see what the son has to say for himself. He doesn't care about what the neighbours think. He's not worried about any of that. He just wants to be with his boy again. He is filled with compassion.

Try and picture this scene in your head. The boy is slowly walking towards the house, terrified of what is about to happen. The father is sprinting at top speed towards him.

They are getting closer and closer. The boy's heart is pumping now. He is bracing himself for the full force of his dad's rage against him for his utter stupidity...

But instead he is swamped by love.

The exact words Jesus about what the father does are: "He ran to his son, threw his arms round him and kissed him". It is the last thing the son was expecting. It was the last thing he deserved; but that hug must have felt amazing.

The younger son tries to get out the speech he has prepared, but he just can't finish it. It's a comedy moment. His dad is hugging and kissing. The boy can't get a word in edgeways, let alone his "I'm not worthy" speech.

It is as if the father is saying: "Shut up and let me embrace you".

And the point of the story is…

that is how Jesus welcomes sinners.

Remember who is in the crowd as Jesus tells this story? Sinners and tax collectors are all around Him. They are the scum; the losers; the prostitutes; the failures; and he is looking at them, saying: "In the same way I welcome you".

When Jesus sees sinners, his heart is filled with compassion.
He runs to them and throws his arms around them. It is utterly extraordinary.

Have you experienced this?

Here's the thing. Have you experienced that mind-blowing welcome for yourself? Because this is what it means to be a real Christian.

It means thinking carefully about what we really deserve from God. We have dumped him to pursue our dreams. We have treated him like a piece of rubbish. We have done a terrible thing. It is pretty clear that God should be utterly furious with us. And that's a terrifying thought.

Several hundred years ago a famous monk called Martin Luther understood the truth of this. He was terrified at the thought of coming to God. He said:

> ***I was utterly terror stricken. Who am I that I should lift my eyes or raise my hands to the divine majesty. I am dust and ashes and full of sin.***

That is how the younger son felt on his way home.

When we feel like that, then the welcome of Jesus becomes totally amazing. Despite what you have done, Jesus stands willing and ready to throw his arms round you and welcome you home. So when Martin Luther finally experienced the welcome of Jesus, he said:

> ***I felt I had gone through the doors of paradise.***

Think

How do you feel about being welcomed by Jesus? Is it something that amazes you, or are you not bothered? If it doesn't particularly bother you, perhaps it's because you haven't properly seen what you're like inside?

Take a minute to think about what you deserve from Jesus. The more we see what we deserve, the more amazing the welcome becomes. Talk to him about it now.

We need to go back to the story, because it gets even better!

A transforming welcome

We have already seen that this is a wonderful welcome, but look more closely and we'll find it gets even better...

Remember the state the son is in as he returns home. He has come straight from the pig sty. He's covered in filth; worse than that—it is pig filth. That means he is unclean according to the law. He also stinks. It would definitely be wise to keep your distance. God's law says if you touch someone who is unclean, you become unclean yourself.

But what does his dad do? Does he say: "Go get yourself cleaned up son, then I will shake your hand"?

Or perhaps: "Go and spend seven days getting yourself ritually clean, then I will welcome you into my house"?

No, no, and a thousand times no.

The boy needs to do nothing… the father does everything.

The father throws his arms round his filthy son. He kisses his filthy son. He welcomes his filthy son. The result is obvious. The father now becomes filthy. In order to welcome his son, the father has to become unclean. What a welcome! The father is not ashamed to share the disgrace of his boy's polluted foulness.

But see what happens to the son next!

The father said to his servants: "Quick! Bring the best robe and put it on him. Put a ring on his finger and sandals on his feet."

The filth of the son is covered with a robe. Hang on a moment. Not just a robe. He is clothed in the best robe. He is given a ring; that is, the family ring, the mark of a son. This is so beautiful.

In that one moment the boy is immediately transformed to the position of son again. He had tried to say: "I am no longer worthy to be called your son", but his dad had other ideas. And the transformation takes place the moment the boy gets home.

It's not something the boy does to himself. He doesn't clean himself up. He doesn't clothe himself in fresh new robes. He doesn't even have to prove himself. He is swamped by love and immediately made a son.

Let me spell out again what has happened. The father has become filthy and the son is dressed in the best robe. What a swap!

The point of this story is...

that is how Jesus welcomes sinners.

Have you experienced this?

Our sin (dumping God, pursuing the dream) makes us filthy in God's eyes. We are in a complete and utter mess.

What does Jesus say to us? Does he say: "Get yourselves clean and then I will welcome you"?

Does he say: "Go to church, give your money, say your prayers, keep the rules... then I will accept you"?

No, no, and a thousand times no.

This man welcomes sinners. Jesus came into this world to throw his arms round filthy people. He doesn't keep people at arm's length saying: "Don't come too close". He touches unclean people.

There is a great example earlier in Luke's Gospel. A man with leprosy came to Jesus. According to God's law leprosy made him an unclean man. If anyone touched someone with leprosy, they also became unclean. They were untouchable. What did Jesus do? Jesus reached out his hand and touched the man. (You can read the whole story for yourself—it's in chapter 5 v 12-13.)

There it is. That's Jesus. That's how he welcomes people. He willingly takes upon himself the filth and the dirt of human sin. He becomes sin. He becomes unclean, just like the father in our story. What a welcome!

How? How can this be? How can this be right?

It all becomes clear when you look at the cross where Jesus died. On the cross he was being punished for filthy sin. Not his own; he had none. He was perfectly clean in every way. But in order to welcome sinners, he chose to become unclean. He willingly took our filth; he took the punishment that sinners deserve. There's no other way for sinners to be welcomed. He stretched out his arms and died.

The swap

Look at how this is explained in another part of the Bible:

> ***God made him who had no sin***
> *(that is talking about Jesus; "no sin" means perfectly clean in God's eyes)*
> ***to be sin for us,***
> *(he became filthy with sin—amazing but true)*
> ***so that in him we might become the righteousness of God.***
> *(the result is that sinners are made righteous; that means CLEAN!!)*
>
> *2 Corinthians 5 v 21*

Jesus became dirty; sinners become clean. That is the swap at the heart of what it means to be a Christian.

Then he rose from the dead, and is alive today, ready to welcome anyone who will come to him.

The result is incredible. Unclean people are immediately clothed as children of God. They are immediately welcomed into the family.

This means we must chuck away all those ideas that Jesus only welcomes good people, or nice people, or churchy, or religious people.

He welcomes sinners and he completely transforms them.

This is what happens the moment anyone comes to Jesus. It doesn't matter what you have done. It doesn't matter how far you have run. It doesn't matter how seriously you've messed up. The arms of Jesus are open wide to welcome you. He'll take your filth and dress you in the best robe. He will do it all.

Come to him

So here's the thing. Have you come to him yet?

And if you haven't, what are you waiting for? Why not stop and do it now? You can do it simply by speaking to him. Admit the ways in which you have dumped him. You could use the words of the younger son in verse 21: "I am not worthy to be called your son". Ask him to welcome you. Ask him to take away your filthy sin. Ask him to transform you into one of his children. And he will. He really will, because this man welcomes sinners.

This is such a relief if you can get it into your brain. If we had to clean ourselves up, we could never be sure we had done enough. How could we ever make up for all the times we have dumped him? How can we know if he loves us?

But he has done it all.

And if you have already come to him, then you are now clean. You are already clothed in the best robe. You are already wearing the family ring.

Take a moment to let that sink in. You are no longer filthy. Jesus has taken it away. It is a mind-blowing welcome. Talk to Jesus about it now. Thank him. Praise him.

Imagine the younger son a week later stressing about whether his dad loved him or not. You would say to him: "Don't be ridiculous! He welcomed you home when you were in a right mess. Remember the hug; remember the kisses; remember the new robe. Get a grip; you are totally secure; there is no way he is going to chuck you out. It's obvious!"

Yet, the weird thing is that loads of Christians act just like that. They freak out because they think God is suddenly going to change his mind and be angry. They think of stuff from the past and begin to panic. If that's you, can I give you some advice?

Chill out.

Remember the welcome; remember the hug; remember the cross where Jesus died for all your sin. Believe. You are totally secure. You are a son or daughter of God.

He welcomed you when you were a sinner. You are now his precious child. Wow!

It is a joyful welcome

And it just keeps getting better for the younger son. Not only is he welcomed, and transformed, he finds himself at the centre of a major party—held in his honour! You can hear the joy bursting out of the dad as he says:

> ***Bring the fattened calf and kill it. Let's have a feast and celebrate. For this son of mine was dead and is alive again; he was lost and is found.***

The father is not ashamed of his son; he is not embarrassed; he is not disappointed; he's just exploding with joy. You can imagine the neighbours gossiping about it. "What does he think he's doing?" "If I were him, I would have shown that ungrateful little wretch the door".

It was shocking to welcome him in the first place. To throw a massive welcome party is just completely over the top.

But this is the day the father has been dreaming of. This is what brings the father joy. His son was lost but now he's found again; he was dead but now he's alive. What better reason to celebrate?

Guess what?

That is how Jesus welcomes sinners.

He doesn't do it because he has to; like a grumpy five-year-old being forced to eat brussel sprouts. Jesus welcomes sinners because it brings him enormous joy. He loves welcoming sinners. That was the whole reason he came into this world. He rejoices when lost people are found.

If you have come to Jesus, he is not just "putting up with you". He is rejoicing over you. He is celebrating over you. He's not ashamed of you, or embarrassed by you. You bring him joy. You do not have to earn your place. You do not have to prove yourself. You simply have to come to him—straight from the pigsty. Just the way you are. The welcome that Jesus gives is like nothing else on earth.

Some people think that being a Christian will make life miserable. It will mean leaving behind all the fun and freedom. It will make life *boring*.

Imagine going up to the younger son in the middle of that party and saying that to him! "It must be really miserable being back home. You must be gutted after all the fun you were having in that pig sty, starving to death. What a shame for you to have to abandon your dreams and come back to your father. It is such a pity."

He would laugh in your face. Life has never been so good. Food has never been so tasty. His smile has never been bigger. It is incredible. At last he's found the satisfaction he had been dreaming of. His daydream failed to deliver. Incredibly, he has found the joy and freedom he was looking for in the place he least expected to find it—back home with his father! Who would have thought it?!

Here's the point:

The JOY you are pursuing is actually found in Jesus. It's found in being welcomed by him. It's found in being transformed by him. Life with Jesus is life as it is meant to be lived. Who would have thought it?!

Have you been welcomed by Jesus?

Is this a reality for you?

Do you ever worry that he doesn't love you?

Do you ever feel like you have to clean yourself up?

Do you know the joy of being welcomed into his family?

Talk to God about your answer to these questions...

Chapter Four:
Missing the party

Meanwhile, the older son was in the field. When he came near the house, he heard music and dancing. So he called one of the servants and asked him what was going on. "Your brother has come," he replied, "and your father has killed the fattened calf because he has him back safe and sound."

The older brother became angry and refused to go in. So his father went out and pleaded with him. But he answered his father, "Look! All these years I've been slaving for you and never disobeyed your orders. Yet you never gave me even a young goat so I could celebrate with my friends. But when this son of yours who has squandered your property with prostitutes comes home, you kill the fattened calf for him!"

"My son," the father said, "you are always with me, and everything I have is yours. But we had to celebrate and be glad, because this brother of yours was dead and is alive again; he was lost and is found." *Luke 15 v 25-31*

It would have been the perfect place to finish the story. The younger son has come home. The father has welcomed him. The party is in full swing. It looks like the classic "happily ever after" ending. The ultimate in "feel good" movies.

But Jesus has other ideas. He is not finished yet. This story is not designed to leave us with a nice, fuzzy glow, like watching some Disney film. It has an explosive ending that will leave us feeling uncomfortable.

Because Jesus is exposing a deadly attitude that lurks in our hearts. And when he shows us what is there, it's devastating. In fact, don't just watch what happens; as we look at the story, allow Jesus to examine your heart and see what's hidden there.

It might make you shift uneasily in your seat, but remember this: Jesus only shows us what we are really like because he wants to heal us. He's not out to crush people; he wants to lovingly restore us. If you go to a doctor and they tell you there's a serious problem, they're not being harsh. It isn't supposed to send you away feeling rubbish. It's for your own good, so that things can be put right.

Jesus is like a doctor, showing up a problem in our hearts. He does it so we can be changed.

Stop for a minute and think about whether you are willing for Jesus to show up wrong attitudes in your heart. Are you willing to be changed by him? Why not talk to him about it now...?

The devoted son?

So far we've focused our attention on the younger son and his dad. But there is another member of the family; the older son. He comes back into the story at the end.

Meanwhile the older son was in the field.

In many ways he's flawless. He's in the field working hard for his father. He gets up each day and goes to work. He sweats in the heat of the sun. He comes home each evening exhausted from his labour.

He's the absolute opposite of his little waste-of-space brother. When his brother was grabbing, he was working. When his brother was leaving, he was working. When his brother was wasting, he was working. He looks like the perfect boy, responsible, hard working and trustworthy.

You can imagine the neighbours saying: "You must be very proud of your eldest boy. At least you have one son who is devoted to you." He is quite a guy.

Despite all of that there is a problem with this older son. A dangerous and deadly problem. There is no way of telling just by looking at him. You can't spot it with the naked eye. It's a problem that lies buried deep in his heart. That's what makes it so deadly.

Outwardly he looked fantastic, but inside his heart was rotting.

When we bought our house, everything looked great. But under the floor in the lounge dry rot was eating away the beams. We had no idea about it. We carried on quite happily. That is, until the floor began to cave in. At that point you might think I would do something. But actually I tried to ignore it and pretend everything was ok. The beams kept rotting; the floor kept on sinking; I kept pretending. Until it got so bad that I had to pull up the floor boards. Suddenly the real problem was exposed. You could see the rotten wood, you could smell it. It was not a pretty sight. Slowly but surely my floor had disintegrated right under my feet.

The same was true in the older son's heart. An invisible rot had set in.

The younger son's problem is very obvious. Everyone can see what a waster he is. But not the older son. His problem is hidden away from public view... until the day his brother gets home and then it all comes pouring out, and it is not pretty. Suddenly, the floor boards are lifted and everything becomes clear. The stench is awful. Watch what happens.

A temper tantrum

The older son has finished his day's work and is on his way back to the house. He must have been tired and looking forward to sitting down to enjoy a quiet evening in. As he gets close to the house, he hears music and dancing. He is not aware that a party has been planned so he asks one of the servants what's going on. Then he receives the news. It is the last thing he is expecting.

> ***Your brother has come, and your father has killed the fattened calf because he has him back safe and sound.***

A stunned silence from the older son. What will be his response? His father reacted with compassion and joy at the sight of his younger son. Big brother is rather different. His heart is filled with anger and rage.

So intense is his fury that he would rather stay outside than go into the party. This is strong stuff. After all, they are eating the fattened calf in there. We're talking top grub. Once-in-a-year food. The best that you can imagine. But he will not go in. He would rather miss out than share the same breathing space as his younger brother.

An extraordinary thing has happened. Did you notice? The two sons have swapped places!

The younger son who was outside has been welcomed in. The older son who was inside is now the one who is standing outside in the cold. The younger son is laughing and filling his face. The older son is alone outside and going hungry.

What will the father do? Amazingly he does exactly what he did for his younger son. Jesus says that the father "went out" to meet his older son and pleaded with him to come in. There's no favouritism here. The father loves both his sons and wants both of them to be inside enjoying the party with him. But the older son will not budge.

What on earth is going on in his heart? We thought he was the good guy. We thought he was the one you could rely on. Now it is him who is breaking the family apart. What's his problem? What is it that would make him react in this way?

As the older son opens his mouth, it all comes pouring out. The floor boards come up. All is revealed. All the stuff that had been hidden away is now on public display. The problem is exposed for all to see.

And it's not pretty.

There are two parts to his problem: (1) He does not love his father, and so (2) he does not love the things his father loves.

He does not love his father

This is incredible. He had worked so hard. He looked so devoted. He seemed so perfect but in reality there was no love in his heart. That is very clear in what he says to his dad.

Read the words again. You'll get a whiff of the festering mould for yourself.

> ***Look! All these years I have been slaving away for you and never disobeyed your orders. Yet you never even gave me a young goat so I could celebrate with my friends.***

In that one short outburst we can see all too clearly what is happening in his heart. It's all about him. It has never been about his father. He sees himself as a slave obeying orders rather than a son trying to please his father. His work was driven by love of himself rather than love for his dad. There is no doubt he had worked very hard, but it was for all the wrong reasons.

He was working so that he could look and feel good. I am sure he was very proud of himself. Each day of slaving away in the fields was another feather in his cap. Another gold star by his name. You can imagine him comparing himself to his brother. "At least I'm not like him. After all my work, I really must be very special to my dad." In many ways his brother leaving had worked in his favour. It made him look even better! He loves himself. That is what is bubbling away deep in his heart, invisible to the human eye.

The Bible has a name for this is; it is called self-righteousness. If you want a shorter name for it, it means being smug; living your life saying: "Well done me". It's like Little Jack Horner, who sat in a corner, eating his Christmas pie. He put in his thumb and pulled out a plum and said, "What a good boy am I".

That is the older son. "What a good boy am I." He doesn't love his father; he only loves himself.

It's actually quite easy to look good on the outside, but inside to be driven by a self-centred love. That used to be my approach to washing up. I have two brothers and we always used to argue about who should do it. That was until my mum came up with a great system. She put up a chart on the kitchen wall and every time we washed up we put a star next to our name. At the end of the week we got an extra bit of pocket money for each star. Genius.

I was always up for some extra money. I would rush to the sink after every meal. My two brothers were less bothered about the money and simply went and watched telly. If you had walked into my house, you might have been impressed by my hard work and devotion. You might think, there is a boy who clearly loves his parents. But in fact that had nothing to do with it. In reality it was all about the stars and the cash.

I used to enjoy walking past the chart and counting up all the stars stacked up against my name. It made me feel good and I looked forward to Saturday and pocket-money time. Outwardly it looked good, but deep down the attitude was all wrong.

It was self righteousness. It wasn't driven by love for my mum or a desire to do my bit and help with the rest of the family. It was driven by love of myself.

This attitude is an invisible thing most of the time, lurking in our hearts. But it won't stay hidden for long if we start to lose out.

Imagine my reaction if my brothers got the same pocket money as me. My heart would have been exposed. There would have been an eight-year-old explosion. It would have been extremely ugly. My little face, screwed up in rage, spitting out the words: "It's not fair. I deserve more. What about all my hard work?"

That's why the older son becomes so angry. He is the one who has put in all the effort. He is the one who has been devoted and loyal. "Don't people realise? I am the 'good' one, my brother is the 'bad' one. I am by far the better son. What about ME?" That is what it is all about.

He's put on a good act. He's pretended to be the devoted son. But all the time he was in love with himself.

The trouble is you can't fool Jesus—he sees into our hearts. We might fool others, we might fool ourselves, but Jesus sees the truth. And he hates this self-righteous attitude.

He is looking straight at the Pharisees at this point. Remember them muttering away in the crowd? Jesus is going all out to expose them. They are just like the older son. The Pharisees were ultra-religious. They worked hard to keep the rules. They were very impressive. Highly respected. But Jesus can see that their hearts are rotting.

You get a great glimpse of the "pharisee attitude" that Jesus is attacking a couple of chapters later in Luke 18. He tells a story about a Pharisee who prays this prayer:

> *God, I thank you that I am not like other men—robbers, evil doers and adulterers—or even like this tax collector. I fast twice a week and give a tenth of all I get.*
>
> *Luke 18 v 11-12*

It is pretty obvious who that bloke is in love with, isn't it? It certainly isn't God. He's praying about himself. He must be related to Jack Horner. And Jesus hates it.

On another occasion, Jesus tells them precisely what God thinks of them.

> ***These people honour me with their lips,***
> ***but their hearts are far from me.***
>
> *Mark 7 v 6*

Do you get that? On the outside, with their lips, what they say—they look and sound good. On the inside, they are a million miles away from God.

That is the older son in our story. Outwardly looking good, but his heart is a million miles from his dad.

But wait a second. We mustn't be too quick to lay into the Pharisees. Because this is a disease that infects the whole human race... you included!

Think for a minute. Do you try to "look good" because you love God, or because you love yourself? Don't be fooled. They may end up looking the same on the outside, but inside they are totally and utterly different.

Whose eyes do we care about? Do we care what our friends or parents think more than we care what God thinks?

When you love someone, you're happy to serve them just to see them smile. When you love someone, your greatest joy is to do the things that you know brings them the greatest happiness. When you love someone, all that matters is doing what makes them happy. It is not about what you get out of it.

That's how Jesus lived his life on earth. He didn't live for himself and for his own personal gain. Look at what he says:

> ***I have not come down from heaven to do what I want to do. I have come to do what the One who sent me wants me to do.***
>
> *John 6 v 38 (NIRV translation)*

Jesus didn't come to live for himself and to make himself feel good. Jesus was so full of love for God his Father that his one desire was to do what made his Father happy. He was willing to give up everything out of love for his Father, even to give himself to die on a cross.

That is service driven by love for God rather than love for self.

This seriously transforms the way we think about being a Christian. When we are driven by a love for Jesus, serving him isn't a boring life, slaving away, muttering to ourselves. Instead it becomes incredibly exciting.

Perhaps you have never realised that it is possible for your obedience to make Jesus smile. In Ephesians 5 v 10 we are told to find out what pleases the Lord. When you obey him because you love him, it makes him happy.

Perhaps you have never realised that it's possible to be very obedient and yet make Jesus sad. He is not simply interested in what you do. He wants your heart. He wants you to obey him because you love him. He is not pleased with outward obedience that is not driven by an inner love.

The more we love him, the more we delight to serve him.

I am pleased to say that I no longer need a chart on the wall to make me wash up. I have a much better reason to do it now. I love my wife. I love to see her smile. I have discovered that when I wash up, it makes her happy. Now my washing up is driven by love (umm, most of the time…).

That is why a Christian serves Jesus. They love him. They want to make him smile. They don't want to make him sad.

Here is a great question to ask yourself: Why do you do the things you do? Perhaps you go to church—why do you go? Is it because you have to? Or is it because you love Jesus—you want to make him smile?

Perhaps you give some money—is that to feel good? Or is it because you love Jesus?

Perhaps you don't go out getting drunk. Why not? What is stopping you? Perhaps inside you wish you could but you know that you're not allowed to. That is a miserable way to live. There is a much better way. Look at Jesus. Look at the welcome he has given you. Find your joy in making him smile.

Don't settle for a type of Christianity that is all about "keeping the rules". At some point you will have a tantrum and turn away from God. Instead, be driven by a love for Jesus.

Think

Remind yourself often of what he's done for you.

Stop pretending you are such a good person and instead look carefully at the ways you have dumped God. Write them down somewhere. Try and be specific. (You could find Ephesians 4 v 25 – 5 v 21 to see a whole list of things that make Jesus sad.)

Then, with your list in your hand, lift your eyes to the cross of Jesus. Remember the agony he suffered. Remember the nails, the thorns, the wounds. He died on that cross for all that stuff you have written down. He died to take it away. That is how much he loves you. He stretched out his arms so he could welcome you. He has done it all. He has transformed you into a precious child of God. He delights in you. He celebrates over you.

Wow! Will you now love him? Will you try and live your life to make him smile? What a great reason to live.

Hey, guess what. That really is what you were created for. That really is where satisfaction and joy are found.

That is the first part of the older son's problem. He doesn't love his father.

Here is the second part. He doesn't love his father, so...

He doesn't love what his father loves

We already know what the father loves. We have already seen him bursting with joy over the return of his younger son. But that joy is not shared by the older son. That's putting it mildly.

Can't you just feel the hatred when he utters the words "this son of yours"? He won't call him "my brother". He had written that scumbag off years ago. He is not bothered about him at all. As far as the older son is concerned, his brother is history.

Hear the judgment in his voice when he says: "He squandered your property with prostitutes". His father may have forgiven his crimes, but this older son certainly won't.

Perhaps the older brother's thoughts over the years went something like this: "He's made his choice and he chose to leave (not like me, of course). He turned his back and dumped you in the gutter (not like me, remember). He wasted your money (ahem, not like me). He deserves to be ruined and if he ever shows his face in this town again, then I know exactly what I'll do to it." His heart was bubbling with bitterness and hatred.

To throw a party, no, that's outrageous. It's clearly ridiculous. He doesn't even deserve to set foot in the house, let alone have a party thrown for him. And especially not the fattened calf! No! No! A thousand times no!

"What a good boy am I and what a bad boy is he."

In a sense he has a point. That younger brother did deserve a smack in the face. He was a scumbag. He deserved to be hated for what he had done to the family.

But here's the surprise. The father loves him. The father welcomes him. The father delights in him.

And if the older son loved his father, then he would share his father's joy. He would love what his father loves. He wasn't supposed to welcome the younger son because his brother was such a nice bloke. He wasn't supposed to welcome him because his brother deserved it.

He was supposed to welcome him because that is what his dad had done.

Loving his father means loving what his father loves. But he doesn't. He's a million miles away from that.

Again, Jesus is exposing the Pharisees' hearts. They do all the right stuff; they obey all the rules; but they don't love what Jesus loves. They don't welcome sinners.

Of course sinners don't deserve to be welcomed. Let's not get sentimental. Many of these people were dreadful—traitors, scumbags and scoundrels. Of course they deserve to be hated. And yet Jesus loves them. Jesus welcomes them. Jesus delights in them. And so should the Pharisees. If they refuse to love the people Jesus loves, they are just showing how far their hearts are from God. And more than that—it shows that they are the ones who will miss the party.

It is strong stuff, isn't it?

What about us?

If you claim to be a Christian, do you love what Jesus loves?

He loves sinners. He loves people who have dumped God and made a mess of life. He's so passionate about them that he was prepared to leave the glory of heaven to come looking for them. He was prepared to live in this painful world and even die a painful death. He welcomes sinners. Does your heart feel the same thing? Do you welcome sinners? Are you bothered?

Isn't it easy to want your church or youth group or your group of friends to stay just the way it is? It's a nice place to be. "My friends are there. I certainly don't want others coming in and spoiling things." But Jesus welcomes sinners. Do we share his heart?

We live in a world full of lost people. People who have dumped God to pursue their dreams. People who are heading for a terrible crash landing. Jesus loves this lost world. Do we?

In 1956 a young man called Jim Elliot travelled deep into the jungle of Ecuador in South America. He went to tell the Auca Indians about Jesus. They were a savage tribe who had no contact with the outside world. It was dangerous and difficult. Why would he bother? Why did he love them? It was because he loved Jesus, and so he loved what Jesus loves. Sadly, after just a few weeks he was murdered by the Indians he went to speak to.

You would expect Jim's wife, Elisabeth, to hate those people. They certainly deserved it. But instead she continued to love them. She later returned to that same tribe in order to tell them about Jesus.

Why would she do that? She loved Jesus and so she loved the people who murdered her husband.

Loving Jesus will always mean loving lost people. His passion will become our passion. And the more our love for him grows, the more our love for this lost world will grow.

What shall we do if we find ourselves not bothered about this world? I hope you can see that the problem lies in our love for Jesus. Get to know more of his compassion. Remember the welcome he showed you. As you do that, you will begin to love what he loves.

Think

What are you going to do with the rest of your life?

Are you going to spend it pursuing your own little dreams, like the younger brother?

Are you going to spend it in self-righteous religion, keeping the rules and looking down on others?

Or will you share the heart of Jesus?

This man welcomes sinners. Will you join him?

Epilogue

Where do we go from here?

The story Jesus told ends on a cliff-hanger. We are not told what the older son decides to do. We are left with the picture of the father pleading with his son. Many of the Pharisees listening to Jesus that day refused to come in to the party. They refused to love Jesus and be welcomed by him. Their hearts were too proud.

Perhaps, as you've read this book, you have seen that Jesus is pleading with you to come and be welcomed by him.

Maybe you've messed up big time like the younger son. Or maybe you're outwardly rather respectable like the older son. Whoever you are, Jesus is pleading with you to come and experience his wonderful welcome for yourself.

It is a welcome that will leave you transformed. It is a welcome that will fill your heart with love for him. It is a welcome that will make serving him a delight. It is a welcome that will give you a desire to go into this world and tell other lost people about Jesus, the man who welcomes sinners.

My advice? Don't hold back...

Well done for finishing this book, but it would be a shame to leave it here.

You may have some big questions racing through your mind. Perhaps it all sounds too good to be true. Is it really possible that Jesus would welcome me? Is it possible to know him and be brought into his family? It may sound incredible—but Jesus told his story so that we can know it is true.

Take some time to chew it over. Grab a Bible and read the story again for yourself—you can find it in Luke's Gospel, chapter 15. You could also read some more great things about Jesus in Luke's Gospel.

You can find out more by going along to a church or a group that takes the words of Jesus seriously. They will help you find out more about it means to be a real Christian. Can we particularly recommend:

***Start* Bible notes:** These will help you understand the basic message of the Bible—who Jesus is, why He came and what he wants us to do as a result.

***Engage* Bible notes:** For those who want to get stuck into the Bible regularly—great questions and help for understanding God's book.

***A Sneaking Suspicion*:** A great book to help us work out the answers to some of the difficult questions that we all have about God, the universe and everything.

***Hanging in There*:** If you're someone who has already taken the decision to follow Jesus, then this book will help you work out how you can keep going as a Christian.

You can hunt down most of these books, plus some other great resources to help you grow as a follower of Jesus, at:

UK & Europe: www.thegoodbook.co.uk
N America: www.thegoodbook.com
Australia: www.thegoodbook.com.au
New Zealand: www.thegoodbook.co.nz